The Greatest Commandment

E. Neal Cameron

Forward Publishing
Sydney Mines, Nova Scotia, Canada

The Greatest Commandment

Table of Contents

FOREWORD

I have done this brief study for personal reasons. It began as a word of exhortation from a brother and co-worker who asked me how I obeyed the Great Commandment. My answer revealed that, while I did love the Lord my God, I also had some areas of weaknesses. I realized that I needed to find balance in this matter of loving the Lord with all my heart, soul, mind, and strength. I felt the Lord's leading to search the Scriptures to see what they taught about this greatest commandment of God.

I wish I could say that I have mastered and applied everything I have discovered, but I can't. In fact, I believe it will take me the rest of eternity to learn how to love the Lord Jesus with the kind of love He deserves. I pray that, at least, I will be committed enough to Him to make this my lifelong priority in life.

As with all my books, it is not my goal to be scholarly or academic. If there is one thing I want from sharing this study with others, it would be that each reader be stimulated to love the Lord with the love He deserves. May the Spirit of God be pleased to use this simple reflection on the Greatest Commandment as found in Mark 12:28-30 to stimulate you to a greater love and devotion to our Lord.

E. Neal Cameron

1

THE GREATEST

COMMANDMENT

> And one of the scribes came, and having heard
> them reasoning together, and perceiving that he
> had answered them well, asked him, Which is the
> first commandment of all? And Jesus answered
> him, The first of all the commandments is, Hear, O
> Israel; The Lord our God is one Lord: And thou
> shalt love the Lord thy God with all thy heart, and
> with all thy soul, and with all thy mind, and with all
> thy strength: this is the first commandment. (Mark
> 12:28-30)

Jesus spoke these words in the context of a debate with
the religious leaders of the day. The Pharisees and the
Sadducees had joined forces, hoping to find fault with Jesus and His teachings. While they normally had significant
differences, they were united in their effort to accuse Jesus
of blasphemy. They bombarded Him that day with difficult
questions, listening very carefully to His answers for anything they could use against Him. There was anger, jeal-
ousy, deceit, and hypocrisy in their words. They hated Him
and His teaching. Their desire was not to learn from Him

but to trick Him into saying something they could use against Him. If they had their way, they would turn the crowd against him. More than this, however, they could find sufficient reason to kill Him and get rid of His influence among the people of the day.

One of the Pharisees present asked, "Which is the first commandment of all?" (Mark 12:28) While the question comes in the context of deceit and jealous anger, it was an important one. Little did this Pharisee know the impact that Jesus' answer would have on the course of spiritual history.

Jesus did not make up a new commandment that day. His answer came straight from the Old Testament law. He quoted from Deuteronomy 6:4-5, which says:

> Hear, O Israel: The Lord our God is one Lord: And thou shalt love the Lord thy God with all thine heart, and with all thy soul, and with all thy might. And these words, which I command thee this day, shall be in thine heart:

Jesus' answer brings this Old Testament commandment to light in a new and fresh way. It places this ancient commandment before us as the greatest of all God's commandments and calls us to examine it again. Jesus went on to say that all the Law and the Prophets hung on this first and most important commandment (see Matthew 22:40). That is to say, every message the Lord ever gave to the prophets and every law of the Old Testament had this greatest commandment as its goal. More than anything else, God desires that we learn to love Him with all our heart, soul, mind, and strength.

The Pharisees were legalists. They measured the value of a person's spiritual life in terms of what he or she did or did not do for the Lord. In reality, the Pharisee was saying; "Jesus, what is the greatest thing we can do for the Father?" Jesus answer is striking in this context. He told the Pharisee that day that the greatest thing he could do was to love God with all his heart, soul, mind, and strength. The emphasis is on love. This is something the Pharisees often missed. They were so busy following the traditions that they did not have time for a true relationship with God.

Admittedly, I too, have often missed the point of what Jesus said that day to the Pharisee. I have worked hard for the kingdom of God, but have I loved God? The church in Ephesus is an example of this. In Revelation 2, the Lord commends the church for their deeds, hard work, perseverance, and dedication to the truth. In Revelation 2:4, however, He is deeply grieved because, in the midst of all their faithful spiritual activity, they had forsaken their first love. In other words, they had substituted doctrines and service in the place of true love for God. The Lord called them to repent of this terrible sin, or else He would remove their lampstand (Revelation 2:5)—their spiritual light would go out.

The response of Jesus to the Pharisee's question posed shows me that, more than anything else, the Lord is looking for a relationship of love with me. We can define our faith in many different ways. For some, faith is about following a set of traditions and doctrines. Others define it in terms of lifestyle. Others, like me, have made it about service, truth, and advancing the kingdom. All of these are necessary, but none is of the greatest importance. From God's eternal perspective, He is looking first and foremost for hearts that love Him.

Notice that the word "all" is repeated four times in this commandment. We are to love the Lord God with *"all"* our heart, *"all"* our soul, *"all"* our mind, and *"all"* our strength. If we are going to obey this commandment, we must give ourselves completely to the Lord. There must be no distractions. This command leaves no room for anything else. Loving Him must be our greatest and only pursuit in life.

Obeying this commandment is not going to be easy. There will be many temptations in life to distract us. We will have to die to ourselves and the pull of the flesh. Beyond this, however, I have discovered that, if we are going to love the Lord with all our heart, mind, soul and strength, we need to learn how to prepare ourselves to love Him as He requires.

As I began this study, I was experiencing ministry burnout. Physically, I was always tired. Spiritually and mentally, I was drained. My emotions had gone numb, and I could no longer feel anything. It was in this context that someone asked me how I obeyed this greatest commandment. That question disturbed me.

Over the course of the weeks and months that followed, I began to ask myself some serious questions. How could I love Jesus with all my heart if I could no longer feel anything? How could I love Him with all my mind when I was so worn out that I could no longer think straight? How could I love Him with all my strength if my body was tired and worn out? I realized that all my spiritual efforts were not drawing me closer to the goal of loving the Lord. If anything, they were putting me in a place where I was no longer physically, emotionally, or spiritually able to love God as He deserved. To love God properly, I had to prepare my heart by slowing down and learning to be still before Him.

This great commandment has powerful implications in our lives and ministry. Its application will be different for each one of us. For some, it will mean giving themselves more fully in service. For others like me, it will mean slowing down enough to remember Who and why we are serving. For all of us, it will mean dying to ourselves and seeking His guidance and healing in certain areas of our lives.

Over the course of the next few chapters, we will examine briefly what it means to love the Lord God with all our heart, soul, mind, and strength. The topic is so vast that no study can really do justice to it, but my hope is to stimulate thought and meditation on this important commandment. I trust that this study will be a blessing to all who read it. More than anything, however, I pray that it will be a tool to draw you into a deeper, more intimate relationship of love with the Lord our God.

For Consideration:

- What is the difference between serving God and loving God? Is it possible to serve God faithfully and not really love Him as we ought to love Him?
- Take a moment to look at your own life. What is the most important thing in life for you? How does this measure up to what Jesus told the Pharisee in this chapter?
- What is the connection between loving God and preparing our hearts to love Him? Can we truly love God as He deserves if we burn ourselves out?

For Prayer:

- Thank the Lord Jesus that He gave His all for us. Ask Him to forgive you for the many things that have come between you and Him.
- Ask the Lord to show you, in the course of this brief study, if there are any areas of your life where you have not loved Him as He deserves.
- Ask the Lord to forgive you for putting service and other things before Him in your life.

Loving God with
All Our Heart

2

WHERE YOUR TREASURE IS

Anyone who has done a study on the differences between heart, soul, mind, and strength knows that these various parts of the human being are not easy to distinguish. At times, the heart is considered to be the seat of emotions. Speaking in Romans 9:2, for example, Paul said about the believers in Rome, "That I have great heaviness and continual sorrow in my heart." The heart is also a place of reason and intellect. This is clear from Mark 2:8, where Mark tells us that Jesus knew, "that they so reasoned within themselves..." In Psalm 31:24, we are commanded, "Be of good courage, and he shall strengthen your heart, all ye that hope in the Lord." This shows us that the heart is also a place of strength. When we consider all these verses together, we learn that the heart is the source of emotions, thinking, life, and strength. This makes it quite difficult to separate the heart, soul, mind, and strength.

Every human being is comprised of heart, soul, mind, and strength. Although there is a great deal of overlap in their characteristics, we will examine each of these aspects of human nature individually. We will begin with the heart. My purpose in the next few chapters is to understand more fully what Jesus meant when He told the Pharisee to love Him with all his heart.

First, the heart is a place where our greatest treasures are remembered and stored. Speaking in Matthew 6:21, the Lord Jesus said, "For where your treasure is, there will your heart be also." We have an example of this in Mary's response to the events surrounding the birth of her son, the Lord Jesus. In Luke 2:19, we read, "But Mary kept all these things, and pondered them in her heart." The events Mary experienced during those early days after the birth of her son were wonderful and memorable. They touched her deeply, so she stored the memory of these days in her heart. We have all experienced these kinds of events in our lives. As each special moment happens, we store it in our heart where it is kept safely and remembered fondly.

Memories are not the only things we can treasure in our hearts. In Ezekiel 28:5, the Lord God grieved that the region of Tyre had allowed their hearts to grow proud because of their increased wealth.

> By thy great wisdom and by thy traffick hast thou increased thy riches, and thine heart is lifted up because of thy riches:

In our materialistic age, we don't have to look very far to find people who treasure earthly wealth and possessions in their heart. Even believers can fall into this trap. Listen to what Ezekiel said about his own people in Ezekiel 33:31:

> And they come unto thee as the people cometh, and they sit before thee as my people, and they hear thy words, but they will not do them: for with their mouth they shew much love, but their heart goeth after their covetousness.

The desire for wealth and possessions can take a central place in our hearts.

Notice in Ezekiel 28:17 how the prophet also accused the nation of Tyre of treasuring earthly beauty in her heart:

> Thine heart was lifted up because of thy beauty, thou hast corrupted thy wisdom by reason of thy brightness: I will cast thee to the ground, I will lay thee before kings, that they may behold thee.

The people of Tyre were obsessed with beauty. They enjoyed their beautiful homes and possessions. Their women delighted in their jewelry and fine clothes. Their hearts were focused on looking good and giving a good impression. They judged the value of an individual by his or her clothes, jewelry, homes, and physical appearance. They treasured beauty in their hearts.

What we need to understand about the things we treasure in our hearts is that they have a profound effect on our lives and actions. Listen to what Jesus tells us in Matthew 12:35:

> A good man, out of the good treasure of the heart, bringeth forth good things: and an evil man, out of the evil treasure, bringeth forth evil things.

What we store in our heart as treasure will influence how we think and respond to life in general. What we treasure in our heart will influence our priorities in life. For example, consider a man who treasures wealth in his heart. Won't this have a profound effect on how he lives his life? When wealth is the treasure of his heart, he will ignore more important things to pursue what he treasures. What we treasure in our heart will ultimately define who we are.

When Jesus tells us to love Him with all of our heart, He is telling us to make Him our greatest treasure. This might sound simple, but there are many things that can take the place of Christ in our heart. While we have already examined the church of Ephesus in the last chapter, I want to reconsider it again in this context. Writing to the Ephesians in Revelation 2:2-4, the Lord Jesus says:

> I know thy works, and thy labour, and thy patience, and how thou canst not bear them which are evil: and thou hast tried them which say they are apostles, and are not, and hast found them liars: And hast borne, and hast patience, and for my name's sake hast laboured, and hast not fainted. Nevertheless I have somewhat against thee, because thou hast left thy first love.

Jesus told the church in Ephesus that He knew their deeds, hard work, and perseverance. Here was a church that faithfully served the Lord Jesus in the midst of persecution and tremendous difficulty. Jesus also told the Ephesians that He knew them to be a church that could not tolerate wicked men. Here was a church that hated sin and devoted themselves to righteous living. Notice thirdly that this church had tested those who claimed to be apostles and found them to be false. They were a church that knew the truth and stood firmly on that truth. The Ephesian church endured hardships for the name of the Lord Jesus and had not grown weary. Consider for a moment this incredible church. It worked hard, stood firmly on the truth, dealt with sin, and did not grow weary in suffering for His cause. Yet, to this church, the Lord says, "...thou hast left thy first love." (Revelation 2:4)

What did the church of Ephesus treasure in its heart? It treasured faithfulness to the Lord. It treasured and guarded the truth of His Word. It treasured righteous living. All these things were important, but this church was missing something of even greater value. In the midst of their busy service for Christ and His kingdom, they had failed to treasure Christ Himself. Their hearts were devoted to service and kingdom building but not to the Person of Christ. How easy it is, in our zeal for the cause of Christ, to fall into this trap.

Writing to the Philippians, the apostle Paul said:

> For to me to live is Christ, and to die is gain. (Philippians 1:21)

Paul could have boasted about many things in his life. He had done more for the expansion of the kingdom of God than any other man in his day. He probably had a deeper understanding of the truth than any other apostle. He suffered more than anyone else to advance the kingdom of God. What was Paul's treasure? It was not kingdom building or soul winning, although he did these very well. Paul tells us that, for him, to live was Christ. Christ was Paul's greatest treasure. Writing in Philippians 3:8, the apostle confessed:

> Yea doubtless, and I count all things but loss for the excellency of the knowledge of Christ Jesus my Lord: for whom I have suffered the loss of all things, and do count them but dung, that I may win Christ,

Paul's greatest treasure was Christ. He set Christ up in his heart as his most sought-after prize. To know Him and be found in Him meant everything to Paul. He was willing to give up anything to know Christ.

Matthew 13:45-46 compares the kingdom of heaven a merchant looking for fine pearls:

> Again, the kingdom of heaven is like unto a merchant man, seeking goodly pearls: Who, when he had found one pearl of great price, went and sold all that he had, and bought it.

In these two verses, we read of a man who set his heart on one precious pearl. This pearl became his greatest treasure. In order to obtain it, the merchant sold everything he had. To the merchant, everything else in life was insignificant compared to having that one pearl. Like Paul, he considered everything else to be rubbish compared to this great prize. This is what Jesus is asking from us today. Are you willing to give up everything for Him?

Before moving any further in this study, ask yourself this question. What do I treasure in my heart? The heart is the place where our greatest treasures are stored. Is Jesus the greatest treasure in your heart?

I challenge you today to look deeply into your heart's treasure chest. What do you find in that place? Experiences, memories, hobbies, people, possessions, and work may all have a place in the treasure chest of the heart. Where is Jesus in this picture? Is He somewhere in the back, on a dusty shelf beside your high school friends and hobbies? It is not wrong to have other treasures, but we need to make Jesus our greatest Treasure.

Even the great apostle Paul had many things he treasured in his heart. Writing in Philippians 1:7, he said:

> Even as it is meet for me to think this of you all, because I have you in my heart; inasmuch as both

in my bonds, and in the defence and confirmation
of the gospel, ye all are partakers of my grace.

The Philippians were treasures in the heart of the apostle
Paul. You and I will have many treasures in our hearts as
well. Although Paul treasured the Philippians in his heart,
there was one Treasure that outweighed everything. The
Lord Jesus was his greatest treasure and possession. For
Him, the apostle would willingly give up all other treasures.
Can you say honestly in your heart today that, of all the
treasures in life, none of them can be compared to the Person of the Lord Jesus Christ?

If we want to love the Lord with all our heart today, we must
learn to treasure Him more than anything else in our heart.
All other treasures must bow down to Him. The Lord God
must become our greatest treasure.

For Consideration:

- Consider the heart as the place where we store our greatest treasures. What treasures do you have in your heart? What people, activities, and beliefs are important to you in life?
- How do the treasures of our heart affect our identity? How do our treasures define us and who we are?
- What place does the Lord Jesus occupy in your heart? Are you willing to surrender all other treasures to know Him and experience Him in a deeper way?

For Prayer:

- Ask the Lord to show you what you treasure in your heart. Ask Him to reveal anything you treasure that does not bring glory to His Name.
- Take a moment to thank the Lord for the many things you treasure in life. Thank Him for His rich blessings.
- Ask the Lord to help you to treasure Him more than anything or anyone else in life.

3

E N J O Y I N G   G O D

In the last chapter, we saw that the heart is where we store our treasures. The heart, however, is much more than a treasure chest for our most precious possessions. It is also the emotional centre of our being.

Admittedly, we have seen an excessive focus on emotions in our day. While emotions are a natural and healthy part of worship, there are those who place emotions before God. For some, worship is about reaching an emotional high instead of glorifying the Lord. Having said this, however, I want to underline the importance of emotions in our relationship with the Lord God. In Deuteronomy, Moses warned his people about the curse that would come to them because they did not serve the Lord with the right emotions:

> Because thou servedst not the Lord thy God with joyfulness, and with gladness of heart, for the abundance of all things; Therefore shalt thou serve thine enemies which the Lord shall send against thee, in hunger, and in thirst, and in nakedness, and in want of all things: and he shall put a yoke of

iron upon thy neck, until he have destroyed thee. (Deuteronomy 28:47-48)

It angered the Lord God that His people were not serving Him with a glad and joyful heart. Their heartless worship brought His curse on their lives. This verse tells us not only that the heart has the capacity for joy but also that joy is a necessary part of worship and service.

In John 16:22, the Lord Jesus promised His disciples that His return would bring them an unfading joy:

> And ye now therefore have sorrow: but I will see you again, and your heart shall rejoice, and your joy no man taketh from you.

This is the promise of God for all who believe. The day is coming when He will fill our hearts with joy and rejoicing in His presence. This joy and gladness, however, is not reserved for heaven only. It can also be our present experience of God.

Notice how David's heart rejoiced in the Lord:

> For David speaketh concerning him, I foresaw the Lord always before my face, for he is on my right hand, that I should not be moved: Therefore did my heart rejoice, and my tongue was glad; moreover also my flesh shall rest in hope: (Acts 2:25-26)

Knowing that God was with him brought great gladness and joy to the heart of David. "My tongue was glad," he said. His heart rejoiced so much in the presence of God that he could not hold it in. He was compelled to express his feelings in worship and praise to his wonderful God.

The apostle Paul encouraged the Ephesians to make music in their hearts to God:

> Speaking to yourselves in psalms and hymns and spiritual songs, singing and making melody in your heart to the Lord; Giving thanks always for all things unto God and the Father in the name of our Lord Jesus Christ; (Ephesians 5:19-20)

Notice that this music was not from the lips only but "in your heart." Through music, they employed their heart's emotions to worship God.

Paul told the Colossians to express gratitude to God through psalms, hymns, and spiritual songs:

> Let the word of Christ dwell in you richly in all wisdom; teaching and admonishing one another in psalms and hymns and spiritual songs, singing with grace in your hearts to the Lord. (Colossians 3:16)

The heart has the ability to rejoice in the good things God has given. The heart experiences joy, happiness, and delight. It expresses itself in words and acts of loving devotion.

Have you ever wondered what life would be like without the ability to delight and enjoy the treasures God has given us? I have gone through periods of depression. One such period left me emotionally numb. I could not experience either positive or negative emotions. I would sit in a worship service and feel absolutely nothing. As others around me worshiped and enjoyed the experience, I listened without any feeling to the intellectual truth proclaimed in the hymns and choruses we sung. I would thank God for the truth these hymns taught but felt no stirring in my heart.

News that would normally bring joy no longer stirred me. I would take a day off but could not tell you if I enjoyed my day because the ability to enjoy things had died. At this time in my life, I could not delight in God or anything He had given. I felt neither joy nor sorrow. I clung to the truth I knew of God, but I was emotionally numb.

If there was one thing I learned at that time, I learned the role and importance of emotions. God has created our hearts with the ability to enjoy what He has given. It was never God's intention that we merely know the truth without delighting in it. God expects that those who know Him will enjoy Him and His blessings.

Throughout the Scriptures, the Lord God commands His people to delight in Him and His works. Paul delighted in the Law of God (Romans 7:22). The Psalmist called God's people everywhere to delight in the Lord when he said:

> Delight thyself also in the Lord; and he shall give thee the desires of thine heart. (Psalm 37:4)

The prophet Isaiah pleaded with his people to turn away from worldly things that could never satisfy. He encouraged them instead to turn to God so that their souls could delight in God's goodness.

> Wherefore do ye spend money for that which is not bread? and your labour for that which satisfieth not? hearken diligently unto me, and eat ye that which is good, and let your soul delight itself in fatness. (Isaiah 55:2)

We experience emotions because we were created in God's image. And He experiences deep and profound emotion toward us. The prophet Zephaniah tells us that

God takes great delight in His people and rejoices over them with singing.

> The Lord thy God in the midst of thee is mighty; he will save, he will rejoice over thee with joy; he will rest in his love, he will joy over thee with singing. (Zephaniah 3:17)

If God delights in us and expresses that delight in us with singing, how much more do we need to learn to delight and rejoice in Him?

It grieves the heart of God when His people offer Him insincere worship and adoration. Listen to the grieving heart of God as He speaks about His people:

> Wherefore the Lord said, Forasmuch as this people draw near me with their mouth, and with their lips do honour me, but have removed their heart far from me, and their fear toward me is taught by the precept of men: (Isaiah 29:13)

The Israelite's worship of God was mere ritual and heartless routine.

God has given us a heart that is able to enjoy Him and the good things He has done for us. Enjoyment and delight are essential elements in our relationship with God. God wants our emotions to be stirred in worship. He delights to see those whose worship is fueled by enjoyment of His person. Heartless and emotionless worship brings Him no honour.

As I reflect on my own experience of emotional numbness, I realize that it temporarily stripped me of my ability to truly enjoy God. I am coming to realize that loving the Lord Jesus with all my heart includes my feelings and emotions.

To love God with all my heart means learning how to express my feelings toward Him. Some of us have stifled any emotional expression in our relationship with God. We need to see afresh just how much God wants us to delight in Him. Our hearts ought to be stirred as we come to God and reflect on His goodness and Person.

As believers, we have focused so much energy on serving and obeying God that we have often neglected to enjoy Him. Somehow, we feel it would be wrong for us to experience enjoyment in God. What we have seen here, however, is that God expects nothing less from us. He wants us to experience deep emotional satisfaction and joy in knowing Him. He wants our hearts to be thrilled and overwhelmed with satisfaction and delight in Him.

Have you closed off your heart's emotions to God? Do you realize that, in doing so, you have sinned against God? He commands us to delight in Him and to serve Him with joy and gladness. The God who rejoices in you asks you to open your heart to Him today. Maybe your heart, like mine, has become so heavy that it cannot feel anymore. God is willing to touch that heart and restore its tenderness. Loving God involves the emotions of the heart. God designed our heart with emotions so that we could enjoy and delight in Him.

For Consideration:

- What is the difference between seeking emotions and seeking God? Can we fall short of true worship and be content with experiencing emotions only?
- What do we learn in this chapter about delighting in God? Do you delight in Him? Does your delight in God bring joy and happiness to your heart and life?
- Is it wrong for us to experience great delight and joy in worship? What emotions does God feel toward us (Zephaniah 3:17)?

For Prayer:

- Do you feel a hardness of heart today? If so, ask God to soften your heart so that it learns to take great delight in Him.
- Thank the Lord that He fills your heart with delight and gratitude. Thank Him that He gave us a heart that is able to experience its greatest pleasure and joy in Him.

4

MOTIVATION AND

COMMITMENT

So far, we have seen that the heart is where we store up and enjoy our greatest treasures. Next, let's consider how our hearts affect our actions. What we treasure in our hearts determines our priorities and motivations in life. Consider what the Lord Jesus told His disciples in Matthew 12:35:

> A good man, out of the good treasure of the heart, bringeth forth good things: and an evil man, out of the evil treasure, bringeth forth evil things.

What we store in our hearts will determine how we act, speak, and live. This is the teaching of Jesus in Matthew 15:17-19:

> Do not ye yet understand, that whatsoever entereth in at the mouth goeth into the belly, and is cast out into the draught? But those things which proceed out of the mouth come forth from the heart;

> and they defile the man. For out of the heart pro-
> ceed evil thoughts, murders, adulteries, fornica-
> tions, thefts, false witness, blasphemies:

You can tell what is on a person's heart by how he or she speaks and acts. What is in our heart determines our priorities and how we spend our time and resources.

Satan understands the significance of the heart and its role in motivating the individual. Jesus told a parable in Mark 4 about a sower who went out to sow his seeds. He told His disciples that the seed in this parable represented the Word of God sown in the heart. Notice in verse 15 that, when that Word was sown in the hearts of the listeners, Satan came immediately to take it away.

> And these are they by the way side, where the
> word is sown; but when they have heard, Satan
> cometh immediately, and taketh away the word
> that was sown in their hearts. (Mark 4:15)

Satan knows the impact our heart has on our actions, thoughts, and attitudes. He will do everything he can to remove the positive influence of the Word from our hearts. Satan is in the business of snatching away godly treasures. He will bombard us with temptations in an attempt to replace the treasures of Christ with the things of this world.

The greatest motivator of all is the heart. When our heart is stirred, it will stop at nothing. It will make great sacrifices for that which it treasures. King David had it in his heart to build a temple for the Lord his God. In 2 Chronicles 6:7, Solomon spoke of his father's desire for this temple, "Now it was in the heart of David my father to build an house for the name of the Lord God of Israel."

A quick look at David's life shows us how his heart's desire influenced his actions. In 1 Chronicles 28:11 through 29:4, David hired workers, at his own expense, to draw up plans for this temple. He instructed his men and encouraged his son Solomon to carry on his vision. He contributed sacrificially out of his own resources for the project. 1 Chronicles 29:4 tells us that he gave 110 tons of gold and 260 tons of silver for its construction. We can only imagine the value of this much gold and silver. David's heart motivated him to make these sacrifices.

For another example of how the heart motivates actions, consider the apostle Paul. He was called to be a missionary and evangelist. God put a great burden on his heart for those who needed to know Christ. Speaking to the Philippian church, Paul said:

> Even as it is meet for me to think this of you all, because I have you in my heart; inasmuch as both in my bonds, and in the defence and confirmation of the gospel, ye all are partakers of my grace. (Philippians 1:7)

The burden Paul had on his heart led him to endure great suffering. He was more than willing to face chains and persecution to fulfill the call of God on his life. Writing to the church in Rome, he said:

> For I could wish that myself were accursed from Christ for my brethren, my kinsmen according to the flesh: (Romans 9:3)

Paul would willingly have been cut off from Christ if it meant that he could see the Romans come to faith in Christ.

What we treasure in our heart will determine the course of our life. The heart is the motivational centre of our being. It is the place where commitments are made and life goals are set. When the heart carries a burden, everything changes. Priorities are shifted, and people are willing to give everything they have.

What does all this have to do with loving the Lord with all our heart? Those who know Him as their heart's greatest treasure are stirred to action. They are motivated to follow hard after Him. Their heart sustains them in times of trouble and carries them over every obstacle. Like David, with his burden for the temple, no sacrifice is too great. Like Paul and his burden for the lost, they willing lay down their lives. Jesus becomes their priority and passion in life. Obeying Him and walking with Him become their deepest desire.

Take a moment to consider the motivation behind your life. What drives your goals and determines your priorities? What are you passionate about? Jesus reminds us in Matthew 6:12 that where our treasure is, there our heart will be also. When Christ becomes our heart's greatest treasure, our priorities change. Everything that used to motivate us takes second place. He becomes our focus and passion. Hearing Him, loving Him, walking with Him, and honouring Him become our greatest delights. For Him, we are willing to lay down everything we have. This was the attitude expressed by the apostle Paul in Philippians 1:20-21:

> According to my earnest expectation and my hope, that in nothing I shall be ashamed, but that with all boldness, as always, so now also Christ shall be magnified in my body, whether it be by life, or by death. For to me to live is Christ, and to die is gain.

What motivated Paul in his life and ministry? According to Philippians 1:20-21, it was that Christ be exalted in both his life and death. For the apostle Paul, loving Christ with all his heart meant allowing his heart to be stirred and motivated by Christ. It meant having his will conquered by the greater will and desire of the Lord Jesus.

Those who love Jesus with all their heart have committed themselves to Him and His purpose. There is nothing they want to do more than seek Him. Everything they do is for His glory. They will lay down all they have to honour Him in their lives, thoughts and actions. You do not love the Lord with all your heart if He is not your motivation and desire in all things.

For Consideration:

- How does what we treasure in our heart motivate us and influence our actions?
- What do our priorities in life tell us about what we treasure in our heart?
- Take a moment to examine your priorities in life. How do you use your time? What is important to you? What does this tell you about what you treasure in your heart?

For Prayer:

- Ask the Lord to become so real in your heart that He impacts your whole life and what you do.
- Ask the Lord to forgive you for anything that has taken His place in your heart and motivated your actions instead.
- Ask the Lord to give you such a love for Him that He becomes your greatest motivation. Ask Him to help you be willing to sacrifice all for Him and His purpose.

5

INTIMACY

When we accept the Lord Jesus into our heart, we bring Him into our most private and secret place. The heart is where we keep our greatest treasures. It is also the place of our most private secrets. We don't share the secrets of our hearts with just anyone. Because this is the place where we guard what is most precious to us, we only let those people we can completely trust into our hearts.

When we open our hearts to someone, we expose all that is most dear to us. We expose our deepest desires and ambitions in life. We show them who we really are. Intimacy involves transparency. It cannot thrive unless we are completely honest and open. Where there are hidden secrets, intimacy will always be hindered.

When we open our hearts to the Lord Jesus, we choose to expose all that we are to Him. We let Him see our inconsistencies and weaknesses. We reveal to Him our hidden and secret desires. Not everyone is willing to be exposed in this way. Many respond by hardening their hearts and withdrawing from God.

Speaking through Isaiah's pen, the Lord God said about His people:

> And in them is fulfilled the prophecy of Esaias, which saith, By hearing ye shall hear, and shall not understand; and seeing ye shall see, and shall not perceive: For this people's heart is waxed gross, and their ears are dull of hearing, and their eyes they have closed; lest at any time they should see with their eyes, and hear with their ears, and should understand with their heart, and should be converted, and I should heal them. (Matthew 13:14-15)

Isaiah speaks of a people who did not want God to see what was in their heart. Although God already knew all about them, these individuals did not want to open their hearts to Him and His work. Instead, they attempted to hide their attitudes, sins, and motives from Him. They resisted every effort of God to expose these areas and heal them.

Intimacy involves trust. When we give our heart to someone, we place our full confidence in them. We allow them to see what we treasure most in life. We place all that is most precious to us in their hands. To be truly intimate, we must have complete confidence and trust in each other. Many are afraid to take this step of faith.

One day, God called Moses into His presence on Mount Sinai. Moses remained there for many days. The people of Israel began to wonder what had happened to Moses. They thought that maybe he had been struck dead. They were not sure they wanted to trust such a God. They feared that their sin would bring His wrath on them, and they would be consumed. That day, Israel rejected God in their hearts and asked Aaron to make a golden calf to re-place Him (see Acts 7:39-40).

We can all identify with the people of Moses' day. We know that our heart is not as clean as it should be. There are secret desires lurking there that we don't even want to admit to ourselves. Who among us is not fearful of what would be revealed if God searched our heart?

Israel turned their back on the Lord God because they were not willing to trust Him with their hearts. They feared what He would do if He exposed their sin. Loving God with all your heart involves trusting Him with all that is in your heart.

In our spiritual life, loving God with all our heart involves surrendering all we treasure to the Lord God. It means allowing Him to touch us in places no one has ever touched us before. It means allowing Him to see those things we don't want anyone else to see. This is not a comfortable place to be.

In 1 Peter 3:15, the apostle challenged his readers to sanctify Christ as Lord in their hearts. Making Him the Lord of your heart means letting Him come into your heart and examine all that is precious to you. It means letting Him cast out of your heart anything that does not please and honour Him. When we sanctify the Lord Jesus in our hearts, we are asking Him to come into the most private part of our being. We are giving Him control of all that we treasure and value in life. It means exposing everything we have for Him to touch, heal, and do with as He pleases.

Some time ago, I had a test done on my heart. Before undergoing the procedure the doctor came to my side and said, "Legally, I need to tell you that, if you undergo this procedure, you could die. There is any number of things that could go wrong. Are you ready to have the test?" As I went to the operating room that day, I was literally putting my heart into God's hands as the doctor performed the test. There was a risk involved in letting the doctor open up my heart.

This is the way it is with God. He stands before us today and reminds us of the risk of letting Him into our heart. He will deal with anything He finds offensive. He will cut out anything that is not for our good. We could lose things that we have treasured in our hearts for years. Ultimately, it comes down to a question of trust. It is God's intention to heal our hearts, but are we ready to trust Him? Will we give Him permission today to do whatever He needs to do? There can be no true intimacy with God unless we give Him this permission.

Intimacy also requires acceptance. Intimacy will never flourish where there is rejection, judgment, and condemnation. Paul makes it clear that, because of the work of Christ on the cross, there is no condemnation for those who are in Christ Jesus. (Romans 8:1) To illustrate how the believers should receive one another, he reminded them of how the Lord Jesus had received them.

> Wherefore receive ye one another, as Christ also received us to the glory of God. (Romans 15:7)

Writing to the church of Laodicea, the Lord Jesus said in Revelation 3:20:

> Behold, I stand at the door, and knock: if any man hear my voice, and open the door, I will come in to him, and will sup with him, and he with me.

Notice that the Lord Jesus stood at the door and knocked. He wanted to enter. Jesus promised that, if anyone heard His voice and opened the door, He would come in and eat with him. What is the Lord really saying here? The meal they would share was not just about eating; it was about fellowship and intimacy. When we open the door of our heart to Him, He will come in and have deep fellowship with us. We will sit down with Him and share together as friend with friend. We will know His wonderful acceptance, love, and fellowship.

Loving Jesus with all our heart requires opening up and exposing our deepest and most intimate secrets to Him. It means entrusting Him with all we treasure most in life. When we open our heart to Him, He will come in and fellowship with us. Only then can we know true intimacy with God.

Have you opened your heart to the Lord God? Have you surrendered all that your heart treasures most to Him? Have you allowed Him to search out and know your heart? Will you let Him do as He pleases with your heart? We can only say we love Him with all our heart when both it and its treasures are completely surrendered to Him.

For Consideration:

- The heart is where we hide our most intimate secrets. How easy do you find it to open your heart and expose those secrets to the Lord?
- How does opening our hearts to the Lord require trust?
- Take a moment to consider if you are willing to let the Lord do what He pleases with the treasures of your heart. Is there anything you would hold back from Him today?
- Can we say we love the Lord with all our heart if we hold back part of it from Him?

For Prayer:

- Take a moment to surrender your heart afresh to the Lord Jesus. Commit everything you treasure in your heart to Him to do with as He pleases.
- Ask the Lord to search your heart and expose anything that does not belong there. Give Him those things and ask Him to restore your intimacy with Him.

Loving God with
All Our Soul

6

THE ESSENCE
OF WHO WE ARE

Defining the soul is not easy. Let me begin, however, by stating that the soul is distinguished from our earthy bodies in Matthew 10:28:

> And fear not them which kill the body, but are not able to kill the soul: but rather fear him which is able to destroy both soul and body in hell.

The distinction between the soul and the physical body is quite clear in this passage. A similar distinction is made by the apostle John. Writing to Gaius, he said:

> Beloved, I wish above all things that thou mayest prosper and be in health, even as thy soul prospereth. (3 John 1:2)

It is obvious from this that Gaius was a man whose body was in poor health. His soul, however, was in great health. Again, we see the distinction between the physical body and the soul.

In the book of Revelation, this distinction is made even clearer. In his vision, the apostle John saw the souls of those who had been killed for their testimony and wrote:

> And when he had opened the fifth seal, I saw under the altar the souls of them that were slain for the word of God, and for the testimony which they held: (Revelation 6:9)

Speaking of those who were beheaded for their testimony about Jesus, John wrote:

> And I saw thrones, and they sat upon them, and judgment was given unto them: and I saw the souls of them that were beheaded for the witness of Jesus, and for the word of God...(Revelation 20:4)

The slain and beheaded bodies of these particular saints were dead and in the grave, but their souls lived on. From this, we understand that the soul can live independently of the physical body.

What else do we know about the soul? We have already quoted Revelation 6:9 above. In this verse John saw the souls of those who have been slain because of their testimony. In the next verse, John heard them cry out:

> How long, O Lord, holy and true, dost thou not judge and avenge our blood on them that dwell on the earth? (Revelation 6:10)

The souls John saw in his vision cried out. They were alive and able to communicate. Notice also that they remembered what had happened in their earthly bodies. They also asked God for justice. While their earthly bodies lay in the grave, these souls continued to live, reason, experience emotion, and cry out for justice and righteousness. It seems that who we are is more connected to our souls than to our physical bodies. When our bodies are laid down in death, our souls, with their ability to reason, communicate, and seek God, will live on.

In addition, the soul is not defined by possessions or position in life. We often measure the importance of an individual based on his or her possessions and position in life. When the Lord God looks at us, however, He does not see what we see. In fact, he condemns those who reduce the value of life to earthly possessions and position. Listen to what the apostle James said about this in James 2:1-4:

> My brethren, have not the faith of our Lord Jesus Christ, the Lord of glory, with respect of persons. For if there come unto your assembly a man with a gold ring, in goodly apparel, and there come in also a poor man in vile raiment; And ye have respect to him that weareth the gay clothing, and say unto him, Sit thou here in a good place; and say to the poor, Stand thou there, or sit here under my footstool: Are ye not then partial in yourselves, and are become judges of evil thoughts?

The worth of our soul cannot be defined by what we have in life. Jesus made this quite clear in Matthew 6:25 when he said:

> Therefore I say unto you, Take no thought for your life, what ye shall eat, or what ye shall drink; nor yet for your body, what ye shall put on. Is not the life more than meat, and the body than raiment?

Notice that Jesus taught that *"life"* was much more important than the body's need for food and clothes. The word *"life"* here is the same word used for soul. Speaking further on this subject, the Lord Jesus told His disciples in Matthew 16:26:

> For what is a man profited, if he shall gain the whole world, and lose his own soul? or what shall a man give in exchange for his soul?

This world will come and go, but our soul will live eternally. This earthly body will die. At that point, all our earthly possessions will mean nothing to us. The soul has no need of earthly riches. It does not hunger for physical food or need it to survive. It has no need of fancy clothes or houses. None of these things are of any value to the soul. Its value is not measured in money or position in life.

The value God places on the soul is best seen in how He sent His Son to die so that it could be saved from sin and live forever in His presence. This earthly body will come and go. It is a temporary shelter for something of infinitely greater value–the soul.

In the passages we have examined from the book of Revelation, we noticed that the souls of those who had died were in heaven. This shows us that our souls that will go to be forever with the Lord. Also, God promises to give us a new body that is different from our earthly body. It will be a totally new body, unaffected by sin and the corruption of this earth (1 Corinthians 15:35-44). We will not take our earthly bodies with us. They will die and perish in the grave. Our souls are another matter, however. They will go to be in the presence of the Lord forever.

It is hard to imagine a living part of us that does not need to be fed, clothed, and sheltered. We define ourselves by our physical bodies. These physical bodies, however, are only temporary shelters for our souls. God created us as eternal beings and placed our souls in earthly, temporary bodies. The soul is the essence of who we are and must be distinguished from this earthly body.

To love the Lord with all our soul is to love Him with an eternal love that will outlast our earthly bodies and possessions. When you commit yourself to a husband or wife you commit yourself to them "as long as you both shall live." This commitment will only last as long there is life in our physical bodies. When we love the Lord with all our souls, however, we are committing ourselves for all eternity. This type of love will not end with the death of our physical bodies.

The love of the soul is deeper than any physical attraction. When Jesus was on this earth, many people sought Him for what He could give to their physical bodies. He provided food and healing for their sickness. In contrast, the love of the soul is not contaminated by a desire for riches or possessions.

The love of the soul originates in the very core of who we are. It is an undying and eternal love that will continue when this earthly body has been long in the grave. When all the externals of flesh and bone are stripped away, our souls define who we are. When everything is stripped away, what remains is a soul that is defined by its love for God.

For Consideration:

- What is the difference between the soul and the body according to the passages of Scripture we have studied in this chapter?
- How does understanding that the soul is not defined by possessions or position affect how we define and value others?
- Why do you suppose we place so much value on our earthly bodies?
- What does it mean to love God with all our soul?

For Prayer:

- Take a moment to examine the motivation of your love for the Lord. Do you love Him for what you can get for your physical needs? Or does your love originate from your very soul? Ask the Lord to give you a sincere love for Him from the very depth of your being.
- Thank the Lord that our love for Him will last longer than our earthly bodies. Thank Him for the opportunity to remain in this relationship of love for all eternity.

7

THE COMMITMENT
OF THE SOUL

While we cannot see the soul, we have a role to play in shaping and defining its priorities and commitments. The Bible makes it clear that the destiny and priorities of the soul depend on our choices.

Listen to what the Lord Jesus said in Matthew 10:28:

> And fear not them which kill the body, but are not able to kill the soul: but rather fear him which is able to destroy both soul and body in hell.

Jesus told His listeners to fear the One who could destroy both the soul and the body in hell. This tells us that some souls are on a path to hell. On the other hand, in Revelation 6:9 and Revelation 20:4, John saw the souls of those who had been killed for their faith in the presence of God in heaven.

Not all souls will share the same destiny. Some souls will spend eternity in hell, while others will rest in the presence of their Lord in heaven. One of the most important decisions you and I will ever make concerns the destiny of our souls. The Lord Jesus died on the cross of Calvary to pay the penalty for our sins. Sin separated our souls from God. No soul could enter the presence of God without first being cleansed of its sin. Only those who accept the work of the Lord Jesus and His forgiveness can know this cleansing. To love the Lord God with all our soul implies first that we accept His offer to save our souls from sin through His work on the cross of Calvary. No one can say they love the Lord God with all their soul if they have rejected His offer to save their soul.

Accepting Christ's offer of salvation is the most important decision we will ever make. It is not, however, the only decision we must make about our souls. Now that we have come to know Christ and have received His forgiveness, the next question addresses the commitment of our soul. Jesus told His disciples in Matthew 16:24-26:

> Then said Jesus unto his disciples, If any man will come after me, let him deny himself, and take up his cross, and follow me. For whosoever will save his life shall lose it: and whosoever will lose his life for my sake shall find it. For what is a man profited, if he shall gain the whole world, and lose his own soul? or what shall a man give in exchange for his soul?

Jesus gives us a standard to live by in this passage. He told His disciples that, if they were going to follow Him, they would have to deny themselves and take up their cross. This meant that they would have to abandon their own plans and agendas and commit to His purpose for their lives. No one can follow Him who is not willing to leave the world behind. This is a decision each one of us will have to make. Now that Jesus has saved our souls, will we commit our lives and souls to obeying His will?

Jesus demonstrated His commitment to us by His life on earth. Matthew tells us that he gave his life as "a ransom for many." (Matthew 20:28) Jesus chose to give his life to accomplish the purpose and will of His Father in our salvation. He now calls us to follow His example.

A quick look at the early church shows us the commitment of believers to give their life for the cause of the Lord Jesus. The commitment of Peter was clear when he said, "Lord, why cannot I follow thee now? I will lay down my life for thy sake." (John 13:37)

The early church sent Barnabas, Paul, and other representatives to the believers in Jerusalem. Notice what the church said about these men in Acts 15:25-26:

> It seemed good unto us, being assembled with one accord, to send chosen men unto you with our beloved Barnabas and Paul, Men that have hazarded their lives for the name of our Lord Jesus Christ.

When the believers tried to convince Paul not to go to Jerusalem, Paul wrote in Acts 20:24:

> But none of these things move me, neither count I my life dear unto myself, so that I might finish my course with joy, and the ministry, which I have received of the Lord Jesus, to testify the gospel of the grace of God.

Paul was not afraid to lay down his life for the cause of the Lord Jesus. He was committed to live for the Lord and his glory even if it meant physical death.

In Philippians 2:25-30, Paul told the church to welcome Epaphroditus because he had risked his life to make up for what the Philippians could not give him.

All these individuals made a commitment in their soul to follow the Lord, no matter what the cost. They were not afraid to suffer in their physical body or to die for their Lord. What will be the commitment of our souls? Jesus challenges us in Luke 14:26:

> If any man come to me, and hate not his father, and mother, and wife, and children, and brethren, and sisters, yea, and his own life also, he cannot be my disciple.

Jesus is not commanding us to hate our father, mother, wife, and children. This would contradict other clear teaching in the Bible. He is telling us that our love for Him must be much greater than our love for people. We must love Him more than anything else, even more than our own life. Are we willing to leave everything behind for the cause of the Lord Jesus?

As we mentioned in chapter 6, Revelation 6:9-10 speaks about the souls of those who had been slain. In heaven, these souls communed with God, reasoned, and felt the pain of injustice on the earth.

> And when he had opened the fifth seal, I saw under the altar the souls of them that were slain for the word of God, and for the testimony which they held: And they cried with a loud voice, saying, How long,

> O Lord, holy and true, dost thou not judge and
> avenge our blood on them that dwell on the earth?

When these souls were in their earthly bodies, they chose to live for the Lord. They risked their physical lives for His cause. They committed their bodies to serving Him and obeying His will. They willingly surrendered those bodies to suffer and even die for His glory. They knew that, when those bodies were taken from them, their souls would enter the presence of the Lord in heaven.

Although their bodies experienced tremendous suffering, each of these souls had committed to live for the Lord. They would not let physical pain and suffering prevent them from serving and honouring God. These souls made it their priority and goal to remain true, even if it meant losing everything.

Do you love the Lord God with all your soul today? Will you commit yourself to His purpose even if it means the death of your physical body? If you love Him with all your soul, then you will give your life to His purpose. To love the Lord God in this way is to follow Jesus' example, Who willingly laid down His life for us.

For Consideration:

- How often have our decisions in life been influenced more by our physical needs rather than by our soul's desires?
- Will all souls enter the presence of the Lord in heaven? Will all souls commit themselves to seeking God and His purpose? What does this teach us about the decisions the soul has to make?
- Have you committed your soul to seek after the Lord? Have you made it your soul's commitment to surrender all to the Lord today?

For Prayer:

- Thank the Lord for giving us a free will to seek after Him. Ask Him to give you grace to commit your soul to Him and His purposes for your life.
- Do you know someone who has never committed their soul to the Lord Jesus and received His forgiveness? Take a moment to pray for that person. Ask God to reveal their need and to soften their heart to receive Him.

8

PURITY OF CHARACTER

Next, let's examine another aspect of loving Jesus with our souls. The Bible challenges us to keep watch over our souls. In fact, the writer to the Hebrews tells us that God gives us leaders to help us do just that:

> Obey them that have the rule over you, and submit yourselves: for they watch for your souls, as they that must give account, that they may do it with joy, and not with grief: for that is unprofitable for you. (Hebrews 13:17)

Just as spiritual leaders watch for our souls, our enemy Satan is also watching our souls. He tries to influence them to turn from our Creator. The apostle Peter made bold declarations of faith in his life, but he also denied the Lord Jesus three times. Peter understood how easy it is for the believer to fall. He understood the power of the enemy to deceive and tempt. There is a great battle taking place for the allegiance of our souls.

Knowing what it was like to fall prey to the temptations of the enemy, Peter wrote:

> Dearly beloved, I beseech you as strangers and pilgrims, abstain from fleshly lusts, which war against the soul; (1 Peter 2:11)

Who among us has not felt the sting of these lusts in our soul? The enemy would like nothing more than to fill our souls with sinful lusts and desires. His intention is to distract us from the purpose of our Creator and set our souls on a path to destruction and spiritual defeat.

Listen to what the apostle Peter had to say about false teachers in 2 Peter 2:14:

> Having eyes full of adultery, and that cannot cease from sin; beguiling unstable souls: an heart they have exercised with covetous practices; cursed children:

Notice the phrase, "beguiling unstable souls." These false teachers were leading souls away from the truth of God's Word and beguiling them with deception

We are living in a world that has been deceived by false teachers and temptations of Satan. This is not new. Writing in Romans 1:21-25, the apostle Paul spoke of the corruption that ravaged the souls of men and women of his day:

> Because that, when they knew God, they glorified him not as God, neither were thankful; but became vain in their imaginations, and their foolish heart was darkened. Professing themselves to be wise, they became fools, And changed the glory of the uncorruptible God into an image made like to corruptible man, and to birds, and fourfooted beasts, and creeping things. Wherefore God also gave them up to uncleanness through the lusts of their

own hearts, to dishonour their own bodies between themselves: Who changed the truth of God into a lie, and worshipped and served the creature more than the Creator, who is blessed for ever. Amen.

Many people have allowed their souls to be contaminated by the lusts of this world and the temptations that surround them. They succumb to evil desires and sinful attitudes. People surrender their souls to sinful ways.

As believers, we have the obligation to keep our souls pure and right before God. Listen to Paul's prayer for the Thessalonian believers:

> And the very God of peace sanctify you wholly; and I pray God your whole spirit and soul and body be preserved blameless unto the coming of our Lord Jesus Christ.

The apostle Paul prayed that the spirit, soul, and body of each believer in Thessalonica would be kept blameless. We can sin against our souls by allowing them to be corrupted by the temptations of this world. Many have fallen prey to these temptations and have corrupted their souls.

Loving Jesus with all our soul implies keeping our souls pure and free from distraction. It is the great desire of the Lord Jesus to present us to his Father as a spotless, pure bride. Listen to Paul's challenge to the believers in Ephesus:

> Husbands, love your wives, even as Christ also loved the church, and gave himself for it; That he might sanctify and cleanse it with the washing of water by the word, That he might present it to himself a glorious church, not having spot, or wrinkle,

> or any such thing; but that it should be holy and without blemish. (Ephesians 5:25-27)

Christ gave Himself for us so He could cleanse us. He desires to present us to the Father as holy and blameless. Remember, it is our souls that will enter the presence of God in heaven.

The apostle Peter writes in 2 Peter 3:14:

> Wherefore, beloved, seeing that ye look for such things, be diligent that ye may be found of him in peace, without spot, and blameless.

In light of what the Lord Jesus has done, it is our obligation to keep our souls pure and blameless. This process will require a specific effort on our part. The apostle Peter tells us in 1 Peter 1:22:

> Seeing ye have purified your souls in obeying the truth through the Spirit to unfeigned love of the brethren, see that ye love one another with a pure heart fervently.

These believers were purifying their souls through obedience to the Word of God. Peter encouraged them to continue doing this. To keep our souls pure, we must learn to walk in obedience to the truth of God's Word.

Our souls can be corrupted and follow after evil. To love the Lord with all our souls, we will make every effort to purify those souls from all sins. We will make it our priority to keep our souls clean for our Lord. When I married my wife, I promised to keep myself for her alone. This is what the believer must do as well. We must keep our souls for the

Lord Jesus alone. Out of love and devotion to Him, we guard our souls so that they please Him and bring Him great delight and honour.

From the very beginning of time, the enemy has tried to corrupt the souls of men and women by turning them from the purpose of the Lord God and His Word. Loving God with all our souls means keeping our lives pure and free from evil. The Old Testament law required that only lambs without blemish could be offered to the Lord as a sin offering. God expects that, as we prepare our souls to be with Him forever, we will do all we can to purify them.

Loving God with all our soul means offering Him a soul that is pure, blameless, and without wrinkle. If you love Him with all your soul, you will not want to have anything in your life that displeases Him or pushes Him away. You will do everything in your power to honour Him in your attitudes, actions, and thoughts.

For Consideration:

- Can our souls be influenced by evil?
- How does keeping our souls pure and undefiled reveal our love for God?
- How has the enemy been trying to defile our souls today? What particular temptations do you struggle with?

For Prayer:

- Ask the Lord to reveal any way in which your soul has been corrupted by sin and evil. Ask God to forgive you and cleanse you.
- Ask God to give you a desire to keep pure and free from any sin that would defile your soul.
- Thank the Lord that He is able to cleanse and forgive us for the impurities of our soul.

Loving God with
All Our Strength

9

BE STRONG

Some time ago, I was weary from the stress of much service. I remember at that time how the Lord spoke to my heart. "Wayne," I heard Him say in my heart, "you can't give out of emptiness. You have to give out of overflow." This had a profound impact on my thinking from that point on. I had been saturated with the teaching that we always had to empty ourselves and that, at best, we were empty vessels. The problem with this teaching is that an empty vessel has nothing to give. If we are going to give, we need to be full.

This study came about because of my struggle with ministry burnout. I had been giving much to the service of the Lord, but I wasn't being filled. There came a point in my life where I was physically, spiritually, and emotionally drained. On one occasion, I blacked out while driving my car and landed upside down in a ditch. The physical exhaustion gave way to emotional exhaustion and depression. Yet I continued to minister without getting the proper rest.

It was in this context that a co-worker asked me a life-changing question. "Wayne," he asked, "how do you obey the first commandment?" That question struck its mark. As I reflected on this over the weeks that followed, I began to realize that I did not love Jesus as I needed to love Him. How could I love Him with all my strength if I was burnt out and physically exhausted all the time? I could not give what I no longer had. If I was going to love Jesus with all my strength, the first thing I needed to do was to be strengthened.

The Lord Jesus tells us in Acts 20:35 that, "It is more blessed to give than to receive." The Lord Jesus is telling us that He delights more in giving to us than receiving from us. It is important that we understand this. The Lord wants to give. He wants to strengthen and equip us. He wants to fill us with His strength and gifts. It is His great delight to do this for us.

Writing to the Ephesians, the apostle Paul challenged them to be filled with the fullness of God.

> And to know the love of Christ, which passeth knowledge, that ye might be filled with all the fulness of God. Now unto him that is able to do exceeding abundantly above all that we ask or think, according to the power that worketh in us, Unto him be glory in the church by Christ Jesus throughout all ages, world without end. Amen. (Ephesians 3:19-21)

Notice the connection between being filled with the fullness of God and the praise that wells up in the heart of Paul. Receiving strength and fullness from the Lord produces a heart of love and devotion. When we are overwhelmed by the goodness of God in strengthening and filling us, we express this in deeper love and devotion to Him.

In Ephesians 5:18, Paul told the believers, "And be not drunk with wine, wherein is excess; but be filled with the Spirit;" Being filled with the Spirit is not an option here; it is a command. God *commands* us to be filled. Loving God with all our strength involves first being filled with the strength that comes from His Spirit. We have nothing to give until we first receive from God. If we want to love God with all our strength, we must first receive everything He wants to give.

Sometimes, people feel that, if we focus too much on receiving, we take our focus away from God. Yet this is an unfounded fear. The hymn writer John Newton, who lived from 1725-1807, wrote:

> The best return for one like me,
> So wretched and so poor,
> Is from His gifts to draw a plea
> And ask Him still for more.
>
> I cannot serve Him as I ought,
> No works have I to boast,
> Yet I would glory in the thought,
> That I should owe Him most.[1]

For years now, the words of this hymn have struck me. John Newton understood the desire of God to give. He understood that, unless he received from God, he would have nothing to give in return. He made it his commitment to receive as much as he could from God so that it could be used to honour Him in this life. We cannot give what we

---

[1] Newton, John, "For Mercies Countless as the Sands," Grace Hymns: London: Grace Publications Trust, 1978, #15

do not have. We must cry out to God for more. We must open ourselves to receive all that He is so willing to give so that we have something to give Him back.

If we are to love God with all our strength, we must also realize the limitations of our physical bodies. The Psalmist wrote in Psalm 127:2:

> It is vain for you to rise up early, to sit up late, to eat the bread of sorrows: for so he giveth his beloved sleep.

God pours His strength into our frail human bodies. These bodies and minds grow weary when we do not care for them and get the rest we need. The Psalmist tells us that God gives His loved ones rest. If we are to use the strength God provides to its greatest capacity, we need to care for these earthly bodies. If I wear out my body by carelessness, how can I have strength to love the Lord with all my strength? How can I use the gifts He has given me when I am exhausted and overworked? Even our earthly bosses know that productivity at the workplace goes down when the workers are overtired. The same is true in our spiritual service. If we are going to love God with all our strength, we will need to care for our earthly vessels. There are times when we are so overworked and overtired that our efforts for the Lord, though from a good heart, are far less than He deserves.

Loving Jesus with all our strength involves first letting Him give us all we need for ministry and service. If He doesn't give, we will have nothing to offer. As believers, we need to be filled to overflowing. As He fills us, we are renewed and strengthened. God will not only fill us, but He will also overflow through us to others. If we give out of emptiness, we will soon shrivel up. When we give out of overflow, however, we are constantly being renewed. No one can continue to give out of emptiness. We must be filled and overflowing if we are going to continue in service. The prayer of the apostle Paul for the believers in 1 Thessalonians 3:12 was that they would overflow in love for each other.

> And the Lord make you to increase and abound in love one toward another, and toward all men, even as we do toward you:

What is true of love is also true of our strength. We must overflow with the strength God provides so that not only will we be filled but others will be blessed as well.

The strength God provides must be renewed each day. It is renewed as we seek the Lord and His filling, but it is also renewed as we care for our bodies. They are the instruments God uses to demonstrate His strength to the world. To love the Lord with all your strength involves both receiving His strength and caring for the earthly vessels into which He places that strength. To consistently push yourself beyond what your earthly vessel can handle will only diminish your ability to love God with all your strength.

For Consideration:

- Where does our strength to serve the Lord come from?
- Is it wrong for us to constantly seek more of God's strength? What should be our motivation for seeking the strength of the Lord?
- How important is it that we recognize the limitations of these earthly bodies? How important is it that we care for the bodies into which the Lord pours His strength?
- Have you serving the Lord out of your emptiness? What can you do to be strengthened?

For Prayer:

- Thank the Lord for the strength He makes available to you.
- Ask the Lord to give you grace to use the strength He gives you to honour His name.
- Ask the Lord to help you to care for the body into which He pours His strength.
- Take a moment to confess to the Lord that you have not always taken care of your vessel. Ask Him to continue to pour out His strength in you.

10

PERSEVERING
IN DIFFICULT SITUATIONS

In the last chapter we saw that, if we want to love the Lord with all our strength, we need to be a people who are seeking to be filled each day with the strength He so willingly provides.

Serving God with all our strength is not easy. God provides the strength we need, but this does not remove the struggles of life. There is a wonderful story in the book of 2 Samuel 23:9-10 about one of David's mighty men, a man by the name of Eleazar:

> And after him was Eleazar the son of Dodo the Ahohite, one of the three mighty men with David, when they defied the Philistines that were there gathered together to battle, and the men of Israel were gone away: He arose, and smote the Philistines until his hand was weary, and his hand clave unto the sword: and the Lord wrought a great victory that day; and the people returned after him only to spoil.

Eleazar is an example of a man who served the Lord God with all his strength. He stood his ground and defended a piece of land by himself. When everyone else abandoned their post, Eleazar fought the enemy until his hand grew so tired that it froze to his sword. God rewarded his faithfulness and gave him victory. The rest of David's army came back simply to strip the dead of their valuables.

In Eleazar's case, loving the Lord with all his strength involved a lot of hard work and discipline. It meant standing alone when everyone else abandoned their post. It involved pain and suffering for him, but he was willing to make the effort.

We see this same dedication in the life of the apostle Paul. We read in Acts 14:19-22:

> And there came thither certain Jews from Antioch and Iconium, who persuaded the people, and, having stoned Paul, drew him out of the city, supposing he had been dead. Howbeit, as the disciples stood round about him, he rose up, and came into the city: and the next day he departed with Barnabas to Derbe. And when they had preached the gospel to that city, and had taught many, they returned again to Lystra, and to Iconium, and Antioch, Confirming the souls of the disciples, and exhorting them to continue in the faith, and that we must through much tribulation enter into the kingdom of God.

After being stoned in Lystra and left for dead outside the city, Paul got up and traveled to the city of Derbe where he continued to preach the good news and strengthen believers. While I have never been stoned for my faith, I can imagine that Paul suffered tremendously. He may have been knocked unconscious by these stones. He was likely bruised and maybe had a few broken bones. Traveling in that condition required tremendous strength of body and emotion. Paul loved the Lord Jesus so much that he was more than willing to invest all his strength into reaching others with the message of Jesus' love and forgiveness.

Later, Paul went to great lengths to describe the difficulties he faced in his ministry for the Lord:

> Thrice was I beaten with rods, once was I stoned, thrice I suffered shipwreck, a night and a day I have been in the deep; In journeyings often, in perils of waters, in perils of robbers, in perils by mine own countrymen, in perils by the heathen, in perils in the city, in perils in the wilderness, in perils in the sea, in perils among false brethren; In weariness and painfulness, in watchings often, in hunger and thirst, in fastings often, in cold and nakedness. Beside those things that are without, that which cometh upon me daily, the care of all the churches. Who is weak, and I am not weak? who is offended, and I burn not? (2 Corinthians 11:25-28)

You can't read this passage without being struck by the tremendous amount of physical and emotional strength required to endure what Paul endured. Here was a man who was physically beaten and stoned. He was shipwrecked and, for a whole night and day, fought for his life in the open sea. He laboured and toiled constantly. Sometimes, he had no sleep and experienced hunger and piercing cold. All this, no doubt, exhausted his resources of strength. What kept him going? What was his motivation? His love for the Saviour enabled Paul to endure. He is a powerful example of a man who loved his Saviour with all his strength.

Paul's example is not the only one in the Scriptures. The writer to the Hebrews speaks of many other individuals who were willing to suffer and endure great physical hardships for the cause of their Lord. Listen to what he writes in Hebrews 11:32-38:

> And what shall I more say? for the time would fail me to tell of Gedeon, and of Barak, and of Samson, and of Jephthae; of David also, and Samuel, and of the prophets: Who through faith subdued kingdoms, wrought righteousness, obtained promises, stopped the mouths of lions, Quenched the violence of fire, escaped the edge of the sword, out of weakness were made strong, waxed valiant in fight, turned to flight the armies of the aliens. Women received their dead raised to life again: and others were tortured, not accepting deliverance; that they might obtain a better resurrection: And others had trial of cruel mockings and scourgings, yea, moreover of bonds and imprisonment: They were stoned, they were sawn asunder, were tempted, were slain with the sword: they wandered about in sheepskins and goatskins; being destitute, afflicted, tormented; (Of whom the world was not worthy:) they wandered in deserts, and in mountains, and in dens and caves of the earth.

The people spoken of here were ordinary men and women strengthened by God to face the battle. They were tortured, mocked, flogged, chained, stoned, sawn in two, mistreated, and persecuted. They lived in caves, mountains, deserts, and holes in the ground. Their faithfulness to the Lord God required tremendous amounts of physical and emotional strength. They endured all and persevered in the strength the Lord provided. These heroes of the faith show us what it means to love God with all your strength.

I don't know what opposition you face today. We may not face the same opposition as these men and women, but God is calling us, too, to stand firm in the strength He provides. Writing to the Galatians, Paul says:

> And let us not be weary in well doing: for in due season we shall reap, if we faint not. (Galatians 6:9)

Paul challenged the Galatians not to grow weary. They were not to give up. They were to persevere in the work God had given them. As one who has been in ministry for many years, I understand how easy it is for us to grow weary in serving the Lord. Sometimes, the obstacles that stand in our way can discourage us. Like Jeremiah, we may work for years without seeing fruit for our hard labours. At times, people don't appreciate our efforts. Many great servants of God before us have also grown weary. The prophet Elijah is a clear example of this. In 1 Kings 19, after defeating the prophets of Baal, Elijah was physically and emotionally depleted. In 1 Kings 19:4 we read:

> But he himself went a day's journey into the wilderness, and came and sat down under a juniper tree: and he requested for himself that he might die; and said, It is enough; now, O Lord, take away my life; for I am not better than my fathers.

Elijah was a discouraged prophet. He was discouraged because his strength was depleted. He had nothing left to give--either emotionally or physically. In his weakened condition, he was ready to give up.

In His great mercy, God sent an angel to come and provide Elijah with food. That food strengthened Elijah so that he could make a forty-day trip to Mount Horeb where he would meet with God.

> And the angel of the Lord came again the second time, and touched him, and said, Arise and eat; because the journey is too great for thee. And he arose, and did eat and drink, and went in the strength of that meat forty days and forty nights unto Horeb the mount of God. (1 Kings 19:7-8)

On that mountain, the Lord God met with Elijah, speaking to him in a gentle whisper. Elijah's physical strength had been renewed by the food the angel had brought him. On that mountain, the Lord renewed his spiritual and emotional strength and sent him out again.

The unfailing strength of God can be ours as well. If we are willing to obey, God will provide us with the strength we need. He does not ask us to do anything that He was not willing to do for us. Hebrews 12:2-3 challenges us to look to Jesus as our Example. He loved us with all His strength when He laid down his life for us on the cross:

> Looking unto Jesus the author and finisher of our faith; who for the joy that was set before him endured the cross, despising the shame, and is set down at the right hand of the throne of God. For consider him that endured such contradiction of sinners against himself, lest ye be wearied and faint in your minds.

During His brief stay on this earth, the Lord Jesus gave Himself fully to the work of the Father on our behalf. Luke 9:58 tells us that He had no place even to lay His head.

> And Jesus said unto him, Foxes have holes, and birds of the air have nests; but the Son of man hath not where to lay his head.

He knew what it was like to be mocked and ridiculed. He felt the pain of the whip on His back. He was crucified on a cross and endured this for our sake. He gave us an example to follow. He told His disciples that, if they wanted to follow Him, they would have to take up their own crosses daily.

> And he said to them all, If any man will come after me, let him deny himself, and take up his cross daily, and follow me. (Luke 9:23)

Jesus did not promise that things will be easy in life. In fact, He made it quite clear that the opposite would be true. Those who follow Him must love Him with all the strength they have. This will require discipline and endurance. Loving the Lord God with all our strength means walking through difficult places and persevering in troubling times. Yet, in each circumstance, we will find the strength of God that we need.

For Consideration:

- Will loving and walking with God always be easy? What kind of obstacles will we have to face? What struggles will we have to endure?
- How did the apostle Paul demonstrate that He loved God with all his strength?
- How did Jesus love us with all His strength?
- Are you willing to love God with all the strength you have?

For Prayer:

- Thank the Lord for the strength He provides. Ask Him to give you grace to use that strength for Him and His service.
- Ask the Lord to forgive you for the times you have not obeyed or trusted Him to the end.
- Ask the Lord to strengthen you in the struggles you face today. Commit yourself to using all the strength He provides to walk faithfully with Him.

11

SERVING GOD

To serve the Lord God with all our strength implies using the abilities He has given. Paul told the Corinthians that each one of them had received a gift from the Lord to use for His glory.

> But the manifestation of the Spirit is given to every man to profit withal. For to one is given by the Spirit the word of wisdom; to another the word of knowledge by the same Spirit; To another faith by the same Spirit; to another the gifts of healing by the same Spirit; To another the working of miracles; to another prophecy; to another discerning of spirits; to another divers kinds of tongues; to another the interpretation of tongues: (1 Corinthians 12:7-10)

The apostle further challenged the Roman believers to make use of the various gifts God had given them.

> Having then gifts differing according to the grace that is given to us, whether prophecy, let us prophesy according to the proportion of faith; Or ministry, let us wait on our ministering: or he that teacheth,

> on teaching; Or he that exhorteth, on exhortation:
> he that giveth, let him do it with simplicity; he that
> ruleth, with diligence; he that sheweth mercy, with
> cheerfulness. (Romans 12:6-8)

Notice how Paul exhorted the Romans to use the gifts God had given them in proportion to their faith--generously, diligently, and cheerfully. God expects nothing less from us today. If we are to love the Lord God with all our strength, we need to discover the gifts He has given us and put those gifts to use.

In Luke 25:15-30, Jesus told a parable about a master who went on a journey. Before leaving on his journey, he gave each of his servants a certain amount of money. Because he knew his servants, the master gave each according to their ability (Luke 25:15). He expected them to invest what he had given them so that, at his return, he would receive his money with interest (Luke 25:27).

One of the servants buried his money and returned it to the Lord with no interest. Luke tells us that the master was very angry with him for not investing the money and making a profit. The clear lesson from this is that God expects a return with interest on His investment in our lives.

What a privilege we have to be instruments in the hands of the Lord for the expansion of His kingdom. He has gifted each of us for a particular work. This is an honour we dare not take lightly. We demonstrate our love for the Lord God by how we use the gifts He has given.

Imagine for a moment that you purchased a special gift for a friend. You put much thought into this gift and invested a lot of your hard-earned money finding just the right gift. Imagine that your friend received this gift with thanks but put in a closet and never took it out or used it. How would you feel as the giver of the gift?

Some time ago, the Lord showed me a picture of a young child whose father had just bought him a brand new tricycle. I remember noticing the joy on the face of the young child as he rode that tricycle up and down the walkway to his house. What struck me even more, however, was what I saw when I looked at the father. As he watched his son, there was great joy on his face as well. The Lord showed me that day that the greatest way to say thank you to Him is to use and enjoy the gifts we have received from His hand. We demonstrate our love for God by using and enjoying the abilities He has given us.

I want to point out here that loving the Lord with all our strength and abilities is a requirement for all ages. In North America, where I live, many people look forward to their retirement years where they no longer have to work. These individuals may certainly deserve a rest from their earthly work. The fact of the matter, however, is that there is no such thing as a spiritual retirement. When God tells us that we are to love Him with all our strength, He puts no age restrictions on this command.

I have often found great delight in watching believers in their final years continue to offer their abilities and strength to the Lord. It is true that our physical, emotional, and mental abilities seem to diminish with age, but the requirement to love the Lord with all our strength remains. You may not feel like you have a lot to give, but God delights in watching you use the little you do have for His glory.

In the parable of Luke 25, the master gave each of his servants a different amount of money. A quick look around us will show that not all people have been given the same gifts, in the same measure. Some people seem to be given extraordinary gifts and responsibilities. The gifts of others seem to be very ordinary. What we have is not the important thing; it is what we do with what we have.

John 6:1-14 recounts the story of how a young boy's small lunch was used to feed a great crowd. This young lad offered the little that he had, and the Lord honoured it by feeding an entire multitude. Many people with even greater resources failed to accomplish as much.

Jesus expects us to use the gifts and abilities He has given, whether they are small or great. Listen to what He told His disciples in Luke 12:48:

> But he that knew not, and did commit things worthy of stripes, shall be beaten with few stripes. For unto whomsoever much is given, of him shall be much required: and to whom men have committed much, of him they will ask the more.

The more the Lord gives, the more He expects in return. Who among us has not received many blessings from the Lord? We all have one or more spiritual gifts from Him. We have a special role to play for the expansion of the kingdom. God wants us to use whatever we have been given for His glory.

There are two important details I want to emphasize in this chapter. First, as children of God, we are absolutely secure in our relationship with our heavenly Father. Because of what the Lord Jesus has done on the cross of Calvary, I am fully accepted by the Father. God will not accept me more if I serve Him more, nor will He accept me less if I serve Him less. My acceptance before God has to do with the work of Christ on my behalf and not on my efforts to please Him. His love for me does not depend on how I use my abilities. Because I am already perfectly accepted, I am free now to serve Him out of love and devotion. I serve not to be accepted but out of a motivation of love and devotion to God.

The second principle we need to understand is that the God we serve is a sovereign and all-powerful God. He created the world as we know it without our help. He sustains the world without our aid. This awesome and wonderful God is fully able to accomplish His purposes without us. He has chosen, however, to involve us in this great plan of expanding His kingdom. Why would an all-powerful and sovereign God entrust to us the task of expanding His kingdom? It is not because He needs us. Ultimately, it is because He loves us. He delights in giving us gifts and watching us cheerfully use them. He delights in seeing His children marvel at His power at work in them. His heart is thrilled when we overflow in praise and thanksgiving at the miraculous things He is doing through us for His sake.

When my son was growing up, I used to have him help me in my chores around the house. This was not because I needed his help. In fact, his skills had not yet sufficiently developed to be a real help. I actually spent as much time trying to help him as I did in doing the task at hand. Sometimes, his help made the task even more difficult. Why would I ask him to help when I was perfectly able to do the task, with less effort, without him? I was doing this out of love for him. I wanted to spend time with him. I wanted to interact with him. In a similar way, God chooses to use us not because He needs us, but because He loves us.

Loving God with all our strength involves partnering with God in the expansion of His kingdom. Those who love God with all their strength delight to use the abilities God has given them for His glory. They rejoice in using their strength for Him because it is a means of fellowship with Him. They delight in joining God in the expansion of His kingdom. Their hearts are filled with praise as they watch God's Spirit pour through them and use them in wonderful ways for the glory and delight of their heavenly Father.

In my personal experience, I have often found that my closest connection to God has been though the use of the gifts He has given me. I have found that, when I am writing or teaching, God seems to draw close. I experience my closest fellowship and intimacy with God when I use the strengths He has given me.

For Consideration:

- What strengths and gifts has the Lord given you? How have you been using them for His glory?
- What is the difference between serving God to be accepted by Him and serving God out of love and devotion to Him?
- What is the connection between serving God and fellowship with God? How has your fellowship with God been enhanced by your service?
- Is love for God the motivation behind your service?

For Prayer:

- Ask the Lord to give you grace to demonstrate you deep love for Him through how you serve Him with the strength and gifts He has provided.
- Ask the Lord to forgive you for times you have not served out of love and devotion to Him.
- Ask God to show you how you can use the strengths and gifts He has given you to demonstrate your love for Him more.

Loving God with
All Our Mind

12

KEEPING THE MIND PURE

The word "mind" in Scripture refers to the part of us that processes information and makes decisions. In this study, I want to examine two aspects to loving the Lord with our mind.

The first aspect of loving the Lord with our mind has to do with keeping our minds pure. If you are married, you will recall the vows you made to your spouse. You promised to refuse all others and be faithful to him or her alone. This required that you commit yourself to a certain way of life and thought. You turned from others to give yourself to your spouse. Jesus expects no less from us. He expects that, when we commit ourselves to Him, we will demonstrate our love and commitment by rejecting everything that is not pleasing to Him.

The mind is the processing station for many of our activities. Consider for a moment what happened in the Garden of Eden. Satan came to Eve with a carefully reasoned argument. His first task was to get Eve to question, in her mind, what God had said about the Tree of the Knowledge of Good and Evil. He reasoned with her and convinced her that obeying what God said did not make sense. When

Eve was convinced in her mind, she allowed her heart to desire the forbidden fruit. What her heart desired, she acted on by reaching out her hand to take. The entrance point for Satan was the mind. Eve allowed Satan to reason with her and manipulate her thoughts.

Consider another example. Listen to what the Lord Jesus told His disciples in Matthew 5:28:

> But I say unto you, That whosoever looketh on a woman to lust after her hath committed adultery with her already in his heart.

How does this adultery of the heart take place? It is true that the heart is evil and longs for forbidden pleasures. Often, however, what touches our heart must first pass through the mind. If we want to protect our heart, we must first guard our mind. When we allow evil thoughts and desires into our mind, they will soon filter down to the heart.

When we came to the Lord Jesus, we committed ourselves fully to Him. Our heart, soul, strength, and mind were all part of that commitment. I cannot love the Lord God with my mind if I allow things into it that displease Him or come between us. If we are to love the Lord with our mind, we must make a special effort to keep our minds pure and right before Him.

Paul told the Corinthians in 1 Corinthians 6:19-20 that they were the temples of God. The Spirit of God was in them. They had been cleansed and set apart for God and His purposes. Because of this, they were to honour the Lord God in their bodies.

> What? know ye not that your body is the temple of the Holy Ghost which is in you, which ye have of

> God, and ye are not your own? For ye are bought
> with a price: therefore glorify God in your body, and
> in your spirit, which are God's.

Notice that Paul told the Corinthians that they were to honour God "in your body, and in your spirit." In other words,
because we are the temples of the Holy Spirit, we need to
keep our whole being pure (body and mind). We must not
allow anything impure to enter these temples. Loving Jesus with our mind clearly involves keeping our minds pure
and separated for him. There are many areas of temptation for our minds as believers.

First, we must beware of what rises up from our own sinful
nature. The battle to keep our minds pure for the Lord be-
gins with conquering the sinful nature. Even believers can
have evil thoughts and attitudes. We can think evil of our
brother or sister. We can allow lustful thoughts to arise
from our evil nature. Paul speaks of this in Colossians 3:5
when he says:

> Mortify therefore your members which are upon the
> earth; fornication, uncleanness, inordinate affec-
> tion, evil concupiscence, and covetousness, which
> is idolatry:

Those who love the Lord God with their mind must make it
their commitment to put to death the evil thoughts, lusts,
and desires that rise up from their sinful nature and grieve
their Lord. They do this out of love and devotion to their
God.

Because I love my wife and have committed myself to her,
I guard my thoughts about other women and keep them at
a distance. The Lord Jesus expects this from us as well.
He expects that all who love Him will be true to Him in their

mind. They will turn from every thought, attitude, and lust that arises in their mind that would dishonour Him.

Loving from the mind is a very personal matter. People do not see the thoughts of our mind. It is easy to look good on the outside, but it is much harder to keep the right thoughts and attitudes in our heart. To love God with the mind requires deep sincerity. It requires a commitment in an area of our life that no one else knows about.

While many evil thoughts and attitudes arise from our own sinful nature, there is a second source of temptation for the mind. Paul tells us that the sinful mind is hostile to God, "Because the carnal mind is enmity against God: for it is not subject to the law of God, neither indeed can be." (Romans 8:7)

The fruit of this hostile mind is evident all around us. The advertisements on our television and magazines cater to the sinful desires of the flesh. We are bombarded everywhere we turn with the evil influence of this sinful mind. It has found its way into our schools, workplaces, and churches.

In the country where I live, we have removed the Bible from our schools. In its place, we have taught evolution as a way of explaining our existence and made public opinion our authority. Sex education classes now teach children immoral lifestyles. We have taught that "alternative lifestyles" such as homosexuality are acceptable and have legalized homosexual marriages.

Television programs, movies, and books promote sin and laugh at God and His principles. Even believers have been influenced by this sinful, worldly mindset. It is difficult for us as believers to live in this world and not be bombarded by the teaching and thoughts of a mind without God. This worldly mindset grieves the Spirit of God and has no place in the life of the believer.

Listen to what the apostle Paul told the Colossians:

> And you, that were sometime alienated and enemies in your mind by wicked works, yet now hath he reconciled In the body of his flesh through death, to present you holy and unblameable and unreproveable in his sight: (Colossians 1:21-22)

Notice how Paul told the believers in Colosse that they were, at one time, enemies of God in their minds. They were enemies because their minds were not in tune with God. Their thoughts were contrary to God and His ways. Paul described the unbeliever of his day in Philippians 3:18-19 when he said:

> (For many walk, of whom I have told you often, and now tell you even weeping, that they are the enemies of the cross of Christ: Whose end is destruction, whose God is their belly, and whose glory is in their shame, who mind earthly things.)

The ungodly have their minds on "earthly things." Those who love God with their mind will take their mind off earthly things and seek to be holy for the Lord. They will commit themselves to resist the ungodly mindset of the world to keep their minds pure and holy for their Lord.

There is another source of temptation for the believer. Satan will do all he can to fill our minds with impure and ungodly thoughts and lusts. There are several examples of this in Scripture. Listen to the response of Jesus when Peter rejected the idea of Him dying on the cross:

> But he turned, and said unto Peter, Get thee behind me, Satan: thou art an offence unto me: for thou savourest not the things that be of God, but those that be of men. (Matthew 16:23)

Notice that Jesus attributes Peter's thoughts to Satan. In other words, Satan put those thoughts into his mind to discourage Jesus.

When Ananias came with a gift to the church and lied about the amount of money he had received for the sale of his property, Peter said to him:

> But Peter said, Ananias, why hath Satan filled thine heart to lie to the Holy Ghost, and to keep back part of the price of the land? (Acts 5:3)

Where did his plan to lie to the church come from? According to Peter, Satan put it into the mind and heart of Ananias.

In the book of Ephesians, Paul told the church in Ephesus that they were fighting "...against spiritual wickedness in high places." (Ephesians 6:12). He encouraged them, therefore, to put on the "helmet of salvation" (Ephesians 6:17). As believers, we need to have our minds protected with this helmet. We can be assured that Satan will bombard every mind that is not protected by the helmet of salvation with his ungodly thoughts and lusts.

Who among us has not experienced these ungodly thoughts? They come at us in an unguarded moment, like a flaming arrow striking their mark and leaving us discouraged and frustrated. Some time ago, I was walking home after working all morning at a coffee shop on a book I was writing. As I left the coffee shop that morning, I heard an inaudible voice in my head say, "What do you think you are doing? What is the purpose of writing Bible commentaries?" I knew that Satan was trying to discourage me in the work God had called me to do. That arrow hit its mark in my mind, and I wrestled with those thoughts until the next day before God gave me victory.

In the Gospels, Jesus was tempted by Satan, too. Matthew 4 recounts the story of how Satan tried to tempt Jesus by twisting Scripture. If Jesus was tempted by Satan, certainly, as His followers, we are not exempt from temptation. We need to protect ourselves from his ungodly thoughts and attitudes.

There is a great battle taking place for our mind. That battle is taking place because of our own sinful flesh. We are surrounded in this world with ungodly thinking. Also, Satan will do his best to penetrate our thoughts and attitudes.

Loving God with our minds implies taking up arms to guard our mind from ungodly thoughts, attitudes, and imaginations. Those who love God with all their mind have no place for these ungodly thoughts. They want their minds to be places where the Holy Spirit delights to live and work. They keep their minds pure and free from any thought, attitude, or lust that would dishonour Him and His name.

For Consideration:

- Can we love God with our mind if we allow things that grieve Him into our minds?
- What kind of thoughts and attitudes do you have in your mind? What do those thoughts and attitudes reveal about your love for God?
- How does loving God with our mind prove the sincerity of our love? Who knows the thoughts of our heart?

For Prayer:

- Ask God to search your mind to see if there is anything offensive to Him. Ask Him to remove those thoughts and attitudes that grieve His heart.
- Ask the Lord to give you a love that is so sincere for Him that it would willingly remove even the secret thoughts of the mind that do not give Him pleasure.

13

ENGAGING AND
DISCIPLINING THE MIND

In the last chapter, we said that loving Jesus with our mind implies keeping our minds pure. Loving God with all our minds requires more than this however. Writing in 1 Peter 1:13, the apostle Peter said this:

> Wherefore gird up the loins of your mind, be sober, and hope to the end for the grace that is to be brought unto you at the revelation of Jesus Christ;

The phrase "gird up the loins of your mind" is significant. The mind is an important tool in the battle against the flesh, the world, and Satan. How do we prepare our minds for action against the enemy? The Bible has several principles that teach us how to do this.

The Renewing of the Mind

First, if we are to prepare our minds for action, we will need to renew our minds. Listen to the words of Paul in Romans 12:2 when he says:

> And be not conformed to this world: but be ye transformed by the renewing of your mind, that ye may prove what is that good, and acceptable, and perfect, will of God.

Paul told the Romans that they were not to conform to the pattern of the world but be transformed by the "renewing of your mind."

Also, Paul made it clear that the mind of the ungodly person was focused on earthly things (Philippians 3:19). Writing in Romans 8:7, he said:

> Because the carnal mind is enmity against God: for it is not subject to the law of God, neither indeed can be.

These are powerful words from the apostle about the unbelieving mind. We need to remember, however, that this was the state of our mind until we came to the Lord Jesus. To some extent, we are still influenced by the world's way of thinking. Paul told the Romans that they were not to conform any longer to the world's way of thinking. Instead, they had to allow the Lord God to transform and renew their minds.

The ministry of renewing the mind belongs to the Holy Spirit. As we surrender to Him, He will change our way of thinking. He will convict us of our ungodly thoughts and counsel us in the ways of God. As we surrender to Him, our minds are transformed. We begin to see things as God sees them. The sin we enjoyed becomes repulsive to us. Our old attitudes are changed.

As our minds are renewed, intimacy with God increases because we are one with Him in our thoughts and attitudes. As long as our mind is hostile to God, we cannot enjoy intimacy with Him. As He transforms our mind, He also draws us closer to Himself. If we want to love the Lord with all our minds, we must learn to submit to the work of the Spirit in renewing our minds.

The Mind Controlled by the Spirit

In Romans 8:5-6, Paul told the believers why they should allow the Spirit of God to control their minds.

> For they that are after the flesh do mind the things of the flesh; but they that are after the Spirit the things of the Spirit. For to be carnally minded is death; but to be spiritually minded is life and peace.

Paul takes this work of the Spirit a step further in this passage. Not only are we to let the Spirit renew our minds, we are also to let Him control them. When the Spirit of God controls our minds, we allow Him to correct and change any thought or attitude that is not pleasing to the Father. When He convicts us of a wrong attitude or thought, we confess and correct it. We open our mind to the ever-watchful eye of the Spirit of God. We submit to His teaching, counsel, and conviction.

Notice in Romans 8:6 that there is great reward for those who have surrendered their minds to the control of the Holy Spirit. According to Paul, the mind controlled by the Spirit is life and peace. Those who surrender their minds to the control of the Spirit of God will enter into deeper life and peace with the Lord their God. Sinful thoughts and attitudes can only hinder our relationship with the Father. When we allow the Spirit of God to control our minds, He corrects and brings all thoughts into submission to the heart of the Father. This removes the barriers that stand between us and our God. This results in deeper spiritual life, greater peace, and intimacy with God.

Taking Our Thoughts Captive

So far, we have looked at the role of the Spirit of God in renewing minds and drawing us closer to Himself. We, too, have an important role to play. Listen to Paul's exhortation in 2 Corinthians 10:5:

> Casting down imaginations, and every high thing that exalteth itself against the knowledge of God, and bringing into captivity every thought to the obedience of Christ;

Paul told the Corinthians that they were to be "bringing into captivity every thought to the obedience of Christ." Consider the immensity of this task for a moment. How many thoughts pass through your mind in the course of a day? Have you taken each thought captive and made it obedient to the will of the Lord Jesus? This means that when you find yourself thinking ungodly thoughts, you must stop and correct those thoughts.

Some time ago, my wife and I attended a French language school. The teachers challenged us to begin thinking in the French language. I took this challenge seriously. I remember a time when I was shaving and thinking about some things in my life. I realized that I was thinking in English, so I stopped myself and forced myself to think out those thoughts in French. This was a stretch for me initially, but it became more natural over time. Eventually, I learned to think in French. In a similar way, Paul challenged the Corinthians to stop any thought that did not glorify Christ and bring it into submission to the will of the heavenly Father. In some ways, this requires retraining the mind to focus on those things that are godly and holy and refusing those thoughts that displease Him.

When we find ourselves complaining about our lot in life, we need to stop those thoughts, and confess our lack of confidence in God. When we find ourselves thinking evil of a brother or sister, we need to do the same. We cannot experience true intimacy with God if we allow these thoughts and attitudes to continue. We need to make a special effort to take these thoughts and attitudes captive. Loving God with all our mind requires taking our thoughts and attitudes captive so they don't come between us and our Lord.

Filling our Minds with the Knowledge of His Will

Paul's prayer for the Colossian believers can also help us understand what it means to love the Lord God with our mind:

> For this cause we also, since the day we heard it, do not cease to pray for you, and to desire that ye might be filled with the knowledge of his will in all wisdom and spiritual understanding; (Colossians 1:9)

Paul prayed that the minds of the believers of Colossae would be filled with the knowledge of God's will. We have already seen that this takes place through the ministry of the Holy Spirit, Who instructs the believer. The believer is also filled with the knowledge of God's will through the Spirit-inspired Word of God.

Listen to Paul's advice to Timothy in 2 Timothy 2:15:

> Study to shew thyself approved unto God, a work-
> man that needeth not to be ashamed, rightly divid-
> ing the word of truth.

Paul challenged Timothy to study and handle the word of truth correctly. As he did, he would be able to present himself to God as a "workman that needeth not to be ashamed."

Consider for a moment the wife who wants to please her husband. How can she do this if she doesn't know what her husband likes or dislikes? The same is true in our relationship with God. If we want to present ourselves as "approved" workmen, we need to understand the will and purpose of our Lord.

If we are to love God with all our minds, we must fill our minds with the knowledge of God's will. This comes through a careful study and application of the truths of the Scriptures. By understanding His will, we are able to please Him more fully.

The psalmist shows us another reason why it is important to fill ourselves with the knowledge of God's will when he writes in Psalm 119:11, " Thy word have I hid in mine heart, that I might not sin against thee." By studying the word of God and taking it into our minds and hearts, we can keep ourselves pure in the moment of temptation. As our minds are filled with the knowledge of God's will, we know how to respond when faced with the temptations of the enemy. Listen to Paul's advice to the believers in Philippians 4:9:

> Those things, which ye have both learned, and re-
> ceived, and heard, and seen in me, do: and the
> God of peace shall be with you.

The apostle Paul had taught the Philippians well. He showed them the will of God for their lives. They had heard Paul's teaching and taken it into their minds. Now, Paul was telling them to apply it to their lives. Notice the promise of the Scriptures for those who applied their knowledge of truth to their lives. Paul told the Philippians that the God of peace would be with them. God would draw close to them as they took the truth they learned and lived it out. What began as head knowledge ultimately drew the believers of Philippi into a deeper relationship and heart knowledge of God. To love the Lord with our mind requires that we fill our minds with the knowledge of His character and His will. As we apply these truths, we are drawn into deeper fellowship with God.

Disciplining the Mind

In Philippians 4:8, the apostle Paul challenged the Philippians to discipline their minds to think in accordance with the will of the Father.

> Finally, brethren, whatsoever things are true, whatsoever things are honest, whatsoever things are just, whatsoever things are pure, whatsoever things are lovely, whatsoever things are of good report; if there be any virtue, and if there be any praise, think on these things.

We can allow our minds to focus on many things in this life. We can think about ungodly things, such as lusts or sinful practices. We can allow our minds to focus on past hurts and wounds inflicted on us by other people. We can allow our minds to be entertained by things that dishonour the Lord. Paul challenged the Philippians to set their minds on those things that were just, pure, lovely, of good report, virtuous, and praiseworthy. Anything that does not fit these criteria needs to be destroyed and erased from our minds. Believers are to discipline their mind to think on the things Paul describes in Philippians 4:8.

Engaging the Mind

In this context, let's examine one further aspect of loving God with the mind. Listen to Paul's counsel to the believers in Corinth regarding worship. Writing in 1 Corinthians 14:15, he said:

> What is it then? I will pray with the spirit, and I will pray with the understanding also: I will sing with the spirit, and I will sing with the understanding also.

Have you ever been worshipping in church and realized that your mind was not engaged? How many times have we mouthed the words of a hymn or chorus without giving any thought to what we were singing? How many times have we prayed without giving careful thought to what we were praying?

Paul told the believers in Corinth that, when they worshipped God, they were to engage their minds. It is possible to get so caught up in the moment that we disconnect our minds. Worship should involve the mind. This means that we need to give careful thought to what we are singing, praying, or speaking.

Some time ago, I was speaking with a brother in the Lord who was pastoring a church in another community. He told me that, when he came to his church, all they wanted to do was study the Bible. He went on to say that he felt the need to change the focus to worshipping God instead. I reminded him that it was not one or the other. Our study of the Bible should be fuel for worship. The more we under-stand God, the more cause we have to worship and praise Him. Fill your mind with God and His Word. Discipline yourself to focus on the truth of his Word, and you will be motivated to praise and worship God.

God expects that, when we worship him, we do so with our mind engaged. He expects that, when we sing and pray, we do so with our minds focused on Him and the truth we speak. True worship engages the mind.

If we are to love the Lord God with our minds, we must keep them pure. We must also prepare those minds for action. Preparing our minds for action involves realizing that we are in a battle. We must keep our minds from dwell-ing on the sinful attitudes and thoughts that well up in us. We must take each thought captive to the will of God. Lov-ing God with our mind also implies filling our minds with the knowledge of His will through careful study of His Word so we know how to please Him. Finally, it means engaging our minds in worship and prayer as we let the knowledge of God fill our hearts and influence our actions.

For Consideration:

- Does your mind need to be renewed? What thoughts and attitudes do you find in your mind? Do those thoughts and attitudes please the Lord?
- Are you willing to allow the Spirit of God to convict you of any wrong thought or attitude?
- How do you fill your mind with things that are pleasing to God?
- How do you worship the Lord with your mind? Have you ever found yourself worshipping the Lord with a mind that was disengaged or thinking of something else?
- What is the connection between intimacy with God and a mind that is focused on Him and His will? Can we experience true intimacy with God if our mind is filled with unholy thoughts and attitudes?

For Prayer:

- Ask the Lord to search your mind and convict you of anything that is not pleasing to Him.
- Thank the Lord for His desire to renew our minds and bring them into submission to Him and His will. Ask Him to renew your mind. Surrender any wrong thoughts or attitudes to His Holy Spirit.
- Ask God to give you grace and discipline to keep your mind holy and pure before Him.

A Final Word

14

THE DEPTH OF OUR LOVE
FOR GOD

In Mark 12:30, there are two little words that are repeated four times. It is easy to miss their significance in a quick reading of the verse. Consider again what Jesus said in our theme passage.

> And thou shalt love the Lord thy God with all thy heart, and with all thy soul, and with all thy mind, and with all thy strength: this is the first commandment. (Mark 12:30)

Notice first the word "all." This word is tremendously significant, and I do not want to miss taking a moment to deal with it here.

Each one of us has different strengths, personalities, and gifts. I personally experience little emotion, but I tend to be a deep thinker. My wife is more of a goal-oriented person whose concern is to get the job done. These strengths, personalities, and gifts influence how we see life in general.

What is true of our personalities is also true in regards to our gifts. I tend to be a teacher and find great joy in reflecting on Bible passages. The tool of my trade is my mind. As one who has gifts of helps and mercy, my wife empathizes with the pain of others and extends love and support to them.

Even our past experience can affect how we live and what is important to us. Consider the individual who has been deeply wounded by a tragedy in his or her life. To deal with the pain, this individual may suppress his or her feelings to avoid getting hurt again. Maybe you have burnt yourself out physically in your work, and your health has suffered because of it. Now, you are cautious about overextending yourself. I grew up in a family that emphasized the importance of hard work. This has influenced my perspective on life.

Each of us has unique strengths and weaknesses. These strengths and weaknesses will affect how we obey the greatest commandment. Some people will love the Lord naturally with their heart. Others, like me, tend to focus on the mind and the strength. Because I am not a very emotional person, I struggle with this aspect of my relationship with the Lord. We all have strengths and weaknesses. The problem, however, is that the Lord does not give us an option in this command. He tells us that we are to love him with *all* our heart, *all* our soul, *all* our mind and *all* our strength. In other words, we are to love him in all four areas. We can't pick and choose here.

This is a real challenge. Personally, I have loved the Lord with my strength. But I have been weak in the area of loving Him with my heart. The heart involves emotions and, as I said, I have never been an emotional type of person.

I just don't get excited about things in life. How am I to obey this commandment?

In part, the answer comes in the form of the second word repeated four times in Mark's account. The word is the word "your." This important word makes the command-ment personal to me. The Lord Jesus says that you are to love Him with all *your* heart, all *your* soul, all *your* mind and all *your* strength.

This means that my love for the Lord will look different from everyone else's love. Jesus does not demand that I have the same strength as my brother or express my love with the same emotion as my wife. He looks at me and says, "Wayne, I want you to love me with the strength you have. I want you to love me with the emotions you have." Com-paring myself to someone else is senseless. God does not expect that I be the same as everyone else. Trying to be like someone else will only lead to frustration. That is why I am thankful for the word "your" in this passage.

Having said this, it would be easy for me to become care-less in my love for the Lord God. I could very easily excuse my lack of love in any one of these four areas by saying that it is just my personality. I could say, for example, "I'm just not an emotional kind of person," and close that part of my life to the Lord. I could also say, "I'm just not a very intelligent person," and not take the time to study His Word.

Jesus makes it clear that every one of us is to love Him with heart, soul, mind, and strength. Every one of us is ob-ligated to love Him in all four areas. There are to be no excuses for a lack of love in any of these areas. If you are not an emotional (heart) type of person, you will have to seek the Lord's help for this in your life. You will have to ask God to touch this part of your life so that you can relate to Him as He desires. My love may not look like my neighbour's love, but at least I know that God is touching my heart and I am expressing love for Him from my heart.

It is too easy for us to do what comes naturally to us. You can love the Lord with all your strength and not have time for Him in any other way. This will only lead to frustration and burnout. We must learn to find balance. For some of us, this will mean slowing down and spending more quiet time with the Lord to develop our relationship with Him in a new way. For others, it will mean spending less time in study and more time in ministry or simple worship.

It would also be easy for us to find individuals who have modeled love for God in any one of these four areas and base our lives on their example. It is true that God has given us wonderful examples of love for Him in the body. We can learn much from each other and stimulate each other by our examples. It is important, however, that the love we demonstrate to the Lord be our own personal expression. God does not call us to live someone else's life. He has given us a personality that is unique to ourselves and expects that our love for Him in these four areas will not only be growing but also be a genuine expression of our own personality.

As we conclude this reflection, I would encourage you to take time to meditate on this great commandment and what God has been teaching you in this study. Let me offer you three words to help in your personal reflection.

"Love"

Take a moment to consider the word *love*. The Lord God is calling us to love Him first and foremost. This means that everything we do and think should be motivated by love for the Lord God. Do your actions and thoughts come from a motivation of love for God? Do they have as their goal a deeper devotion to Him? Take a moment to examine your day. How much of what you did today was motivated by love for God? Has your life been based on service, doctrine, traditions, or anything else? The greatest commandment is not about promoting truth, extending the kingdom, or maintaining traditions. Instead, it is about love. Love for God ought to be our motivation and desire in life. Is this the driving force behind your life?

"All"

God commands us to love Him with all our heart, soul, mind, and strength. This means that we have a responsibility to love him in all four areas of our lives. Take a moment to reflect on the word *all*. Is there an area of your life where you do not love the Lord God as you should? Take a moment to ask the Lord to heal anything from the past that keeps you from loving Him as you should in that area of your life. Ask God to forgive you for allowing things to block your love for Him. Ask Him to teach you to love Him in that area.

Have you been unbalanced in your love for God? Have you neglected any one of these four areas by focusing all your love for God in only one direction? Ask God to help you to find greater balance. Ask Him to show you where you need to spend more time and energy so that you love Him as He requires.

"Your"

The word *your* makes our love for God personal. Has your love for God been an expression of the personality He has given you? Or have you been influenced by what others expect of you? Do you feel guilty because you don't love or worship God in the same way as a brother or sister? Have you accepted who God has made you to be and the type of relationship He wants to have with you personally? Can you accept those whose love for God is different from your own without criticizing them?

I would encourage each reader to take time before the Lord to consider their love for God. Remember that Jesus said that this was the greatest of all the commandments. It would do us good to spend quality time considering His teaching on this matter and its personal application to our lives.

My prayer is that all who take the time to read this brief study will be encouraged and challenged to love God in a deeper and more balanced way that reflects the personality and gifts God has given to them. May God use this study to stimulate our love for Him.

For Consideration:

- Is it possible to love God strongly in one area and fail to love Him in another? For example, is it possible to love God with all our heart but fail to love Him as we should with our mind?
- Should I expect that my love for God will look exactly like someone else's? How will my personality and gifts affect the shape of my love for God?
- How important is it that we learn to love God in all four areas of our life (heart, mind, soul, strength)? In what areas are you weak? What are your strengths?

For Prayer:

- Ask the Lord to help you to love Him with heart, mind, soul, and strength. Ask Him to teach you where you have been weak.
- Thank the Lord that His relationship with you will be different from your neighbour's relationship. Thank Him that He has gifted you in a different way. Ask Him to help you to love Him as He has gifted you to love Him.
- Thank the Lord that He wants us to love Him. Thank Him that He cares particularly about you. Thank Him that, of all the things He could require of us, His greatest requirement is love.

Thank you again for buying this book!

I hope this Bible study gave you a fresh vision for keeping God's greatest commandment. When we love God with all our heart, soul, mind, and strength, we fulfill the purpose for which we were designed. We can find great delight in our daily walk and our relationship with God. Instead of being a difficult duty, our work becomes a joy when we do it for the Lord. Instead of struggling to do our devotions, we enjoy studying His Word and talking to Him in prayer. By God's grace, let us purpose to love Him with all our heart, soul, mind, and strength.

If you enjoyed this book, then I'd like to ask you for a favor. Would you be kind enough to leave a review of this book on Amazon? Better yet, tell a friend. I would greatly appreciate it! Thank you, and God bless you!

-E. Neal Cameron

OTHER BOOKS IN THIS SERIES

If you enjoyed this Bible study, you may be interested in other titles in this series. They are available in paperback and for Kindle. Check them out on Amazon, or click on the link below.

http://www.ForwardPublishing.ca/

When Sinners Meet Jesus: John Examines Firsthand Encounters with Christ

For His Glory: Cultivating a Biblical Motive for Ministry

Created for Eden

The Little Seed: A Modern Parable

Discovering the Deep Peace of Contentment

Nearing the Finish Line: What the Bible Teaches About Aging

Under His Wings: Finding Assurance of Your Salvation

The Rod of God in the Hand of Man

And more titles coming soon!

Made in United States
Orlando, FL
11 February 2023

29900958R00065